Open Our Eyes

with love and blessings,
ann gurord :-)

In honour and memory of my father, Al Schoelles,
who lived a life of generosity, humility and abundant colour

Open Our Eyes

Daily prayers for Advent

Ann Gerondelis

wild goose
publications

www.ionabooks.com

Published 2016
Wild Goose Publications, 21 Carlton Court, Glasgow G5 9JP, UK
www.ionabooks.com
Wild Goose Publications is the publishing division of the Iona Community.
Scottish Charity No. SC003794. Limited Company Reg. No. SC096243.

ISBN 978-1-84952-502-2

Text and illustrations © Ann Gerondelis

We gratefully acknowledge the contribution of the Drummond Trust,
3 Pitt Terrace, Stirling, towards the publication of this book

Overseas distribution
Australia: Willow Connection Pty Ltd, Unit 4A, 3-9 Kenneth Road, Manly Vale, NSW 2093
New Zealand: Pleroma, Higginson Street, Otane 4170, Central Hawkes Bay
Canada: Novalis/Bayard Publishing & Distribution, 10 Lower Spadina Ave., Suite 400, Toronto, Ontario M5V 2Z2

Printed by Charlesworth Press, Wakefield, UK

Introduction

I often pray with my eyes wide open, filled with expectation. How I long to see God's justice and mercy transforming the very world I inhabit! It's a practice that heightens my perceptions and opens my heart to the wideness of God.

To support this experience, I've developed a practice of drawing while praying – actually recording perceptions in a cyclical process I call sketch-praying. Like drawing water from a well, I work to draw out certain qualities of the world to engage with them more fully. This act of drawing out, extracting, supports a different way of seeing that surfaces in the pages of this book.

Sometimes, for example, I'll draw out patterns and rhythms in the natural world – forests with their visual contrasts and seasons; skies with their infinite layers of changing lights and darks. Or I'll draw out a gesture from a biblical narrative, like God sweeping over the face of the waters, or enveloping God's people in love. Other times, I'll draw out details of the body to explore its role in perceiving the world around it. Drawing the repetitive folds of the ear, I listen acutely to sounds around me. Following the lines of the hand, I attend to my sense of touch. Visual research helps to understand others' experiences. Drawings of desert-scapes, hijabs and letters of the Arabic alphabet expand my visual lexicon, and invite me to see and pray with increased empathy.

The value of drawing while praying expands beyond transforming the perceptions of the one who prays. Through this cyclical process, images take on the role of foundational layers, inviting explorations of the possible. They become prospective drawings of a transformed reality, an answered prayer. For example, a prayer of lament while drawing damaged boats adrift with suffering refugees is transformed into a prayer of expectation as a buoyant vessel filled with healthy, safe immigrants being welcomed home is drawn. In another prayer, isolated religious buildings are transformed to become a cohesive community of God. Finally in the book's penultimate image, empty, hungry hands are transformed into bearers of God's light. The drawings become visual manifestations offering a glimpse into God's holy imagination – a world of justice, mercy and love.

As you open the book's pages, I invite you to explore both the daily prayers and rich images. They are sequenced to accompany you through each of the days of Advent – the season of the Christian church year leading up to Christmas. May they open up a meaningful space for you: to watch and wait for the birth of the Holy One. The descriptive phrase within each artwork lingers after the prayer's 'Amen', inviting reflection, and extending the holy conversation. The prayers developed in response to the writings of Lisa Bodenheim in her book *Disturbing Complacency: Preparing for Christmas* (Wild Goose Publications). They also grew from a practice of loving resistance to increasing global violence, escalating national rhetoric and social anxiety. I hope you'll enjoy revisiting these pages in other seasons, as well – as they call you back into God's presence, to hear God's call for justice and mercy, and to discover anew what it means to be the people of God.

Ann Gerondelis

Contents

As we cross the threshold into Advent, dear God,
open our eyes and our hearts so very wide
that we may behold you anew.
In courage.
In faith.
In love.
Wide and wider still.
Amen

I am near, so near

O God of power, come.
Come in a material way – in matter and body.
Come, as our Hebrew brothers and sisters would say,
as Ruach, a tempest.*
Sweep over our waters,
    our land,
    our hands,
    our hearts.
Both body and soul.
Twist us, turn us with your gale-force presence.
Transform our humanity.
Transform creation.
In the name of peace,
in the name of love,
in the name of justice,
may your kingdom come.
Even here.
Even now.
Amen

 * As discussed in Jürgen Moltmann's *The Spirit of Life,* Augsburg Fortress, and in Lisa Bodenheim's *Disturbing Complacency,* Wild Goose Publications

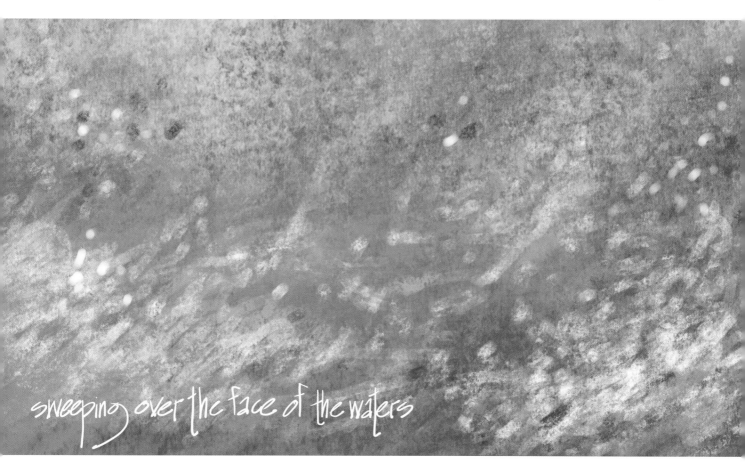

sweeping over the face of the waters

Teach us to breathe, God.
To listen to your heartbeat.
We pray that spirit and body might
be woven together.
We pray with our Muslim friends to know the oneness of Tawhid:
Creation deeply belonging to you,
wholly surrounded by you.*
May we seek not to have dominion over creation,
    but to breathe with it, to preserve it.
May we seek not to have dominion over our neighbours,
    but to breathe with them in support.
May we seek not to define you,
    but to breathe with you, in delight of your wideness.
May we listen to your heart beating in our midst.
May we live into your holy imagination this day,
hands on your pulse,
beating together.
Amen

* As described in the Quran 4:126

breathing with you

O holy God,
in reverence, we vest ourselves in
    tallits and kippahs,
    sackcloths and chasubles,
    suits and dresses,
    hijabs and turbans,
    skullcaps and veils.
Called into community, we practise love together.
Open our eyes to see faithful hearts through our vestments.
Call us together to a place where love trumps fear,
where hate, intolerance, hostility and violence have no place.
    Here, there is
    room for all,
    food for all,
    money for all.
    Love for all.
In compassion, weave our sorted assemblies together
into the Beloved Community that you dream we can be.
Amen

widely welcoming

O transcendent God,
you chose to come to this earth.
In this Advent season,
we wait with expectation for you to come again.
How your voice of
    power,
    truth and
    welcome
    is needed.
Let signs of your love be found in all your people –
we who know deeply that love is stronger than hate,
    stronger than fear.
Come to this earth again in ways that we least expect.
May your presence be the courage
standing up in us,
raising our heads in expectation,
supporting our brothers and sisters
expecting miracles of love.
Again and again.
Miracles of love, indeed.
Amen

standing up

Rough places? Smooth.
Valleys? Filled.
Mountains? Levelled.
Crooked? Straight.
　　All for love.
Power indeed!
In the midst of the wilderness,
your message of justice and peace
has always cried out from your people.
In these Advent days,
give us courage to consider
our role in injustices that surround us,
and our potential power as makers of peace.
May we be so courageous that we let
our bodies be your vessels,
living cries for love,
for justice.
In the midst of the mess,
let choruses of love cry out
and loudly speak power for the powerless.
O God, let it be so.
Amen

crying out

Left or Right. Right or Wrong. Us. Them.
We are different. It's natural to grow apart.
It's easier that way. Yes, easier. Simpler.
In the midst, though,
we sometimes grow too concerned about our own holiness,
even our own type of holiness.
It's easy for the other to become our 'they'.
Over time, they become the unknown.
Is this why love and compassion fade?

O God, remind us that the opposite of love is not hate, but fear:
and fear breeds hate that breaks our communities.
Blow into our neighbourhoods, cities and countries
with a tempest wind.
Open our eyes to new perspectives,
new ways of seeing you at work in our world.
Remind us of the holy work of bridge-building,
of justice and peacemaking.
Heal our brokenness and restore us to a holy wholeness.
Restore us, O God.
All of us.
Amen*

* An animation reveals the drawing process of this piece: https://www.youtube.com/watch?v=M9ZOwZu505g

**Sell your books at
sellbackyourBook.com!**

Go to sellbackyourBook.com
and get an instant price quote.
We even pay the shipping - see
what your old books are worth
today!

Inspected By:mirta_avila

00035865623

G

5623

0003586

healing and restoring

These days,
we are not short on things to follow,
as our numerous pings and alerts remind us.
Jesus's words of 'Follow me' can take on a whole new meaning
in this complex landscape where many things vie for our attention.
We look for signs of the sacred to orient us
    and give us direction.
Sometimes in our looking, we grow too comfortable with
a small definition of who you are.

In these Advent days, when we await your coming,
help us to open our eyes to see you anew in our midst.
As you led our ancient ancestors with a pillar of cloud by day
and a pillar of fire by night,*
we ask that you give us the gift of glimpses of you.
Draw us into your larger-than-life worldview,
filled with unceasing grace, love and mercy.
Miraculously, enough for all.
Draw us into your holy mystery, not overwhelmed or afraid,
but with hearts filled with awe and wonder
at the greatness of you.
Lead us forward, awesome God. Lead us together.
Let it be so. Amen

* Reference to Exodus 13:21–22, NIV

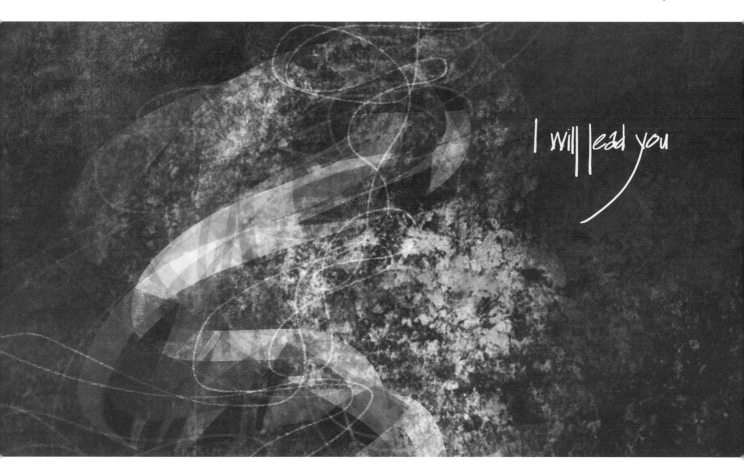

And when you ask how we cared for your land,
O God –
this land that you imagined and called into being,
this land that you were born into
and walked upon with such love –
may we humbly say
that we walked gently through these sacred lands,
one people of God.
Gently moving side by side.
Let it be so.
Amen

through sacred lands

O God who invites:
when we pause, and listen,
our ears can take in holy sounds.
Holy voices.
There are many in our midst
with their unique telling of your peace,
of your love,
of your holy imagination,
stirring,
even now.
Challenge us to seek your many voices,
to draw closer to our neighbour,
and to listen deeply.

Remind us of the power of words
not as weapons,
but as openings to you.
Wide and wonderful you.
Whisper to us this day, God,
that we may know deeply that you are indeed
still speaking.
You have much to say
that your children – all of us – need to hear.
Let it be so.
Amen*

* Pictured is a Muslim greeting in Arabic meaning 'Peace be upon you': As-salamu alaykum

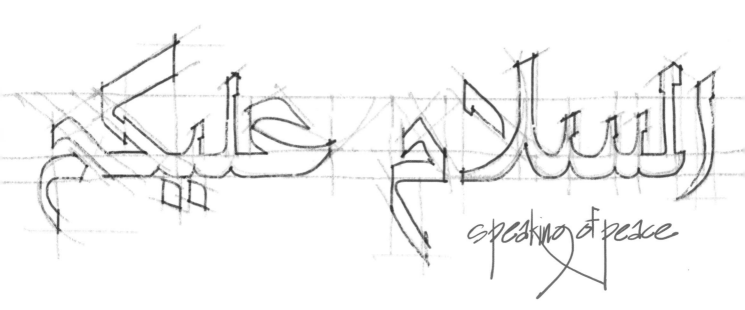

speaking of peace

It's not as if it's invisible,
that line that divides income levels,
haves and have-nots.
Him and me.
Why does one cup hold steeping tea,
and the other stand empty, with some change?
One doesn't care that I'm here.
The other won't leave me alone.
It's just not right.
Look away.
Walk away.
Ease the discomfort of his gaze. Widen the gap.
On a good day, I'd handle this differently.

O God, how we need you here.
You came to lead us, on these streets,
where incomes aren't equal, where fears create distance.
You opened our eyes to see inequalities,
to name them, to erase lines that divide,
to stand for justice.

Come again to create in us a new world,
where there is
    enough for all,
    enough love, food,
    money.
Teach us to look towards injustice, and not away,
to step towards the empty cup, and its discomfort.
To work to know and name injustices in our midst.
To build streets and neighbourhoods
where inequities are diminishing,
where trust is building,
where we are becoming together
the brothers and sisters
that you dream we can be.
O God, let it be so.
Amen

righting injustice

Boundaries. Borders.
Invisible lines separating
people, communities, nations.
'We' are this. 'They' are that.
Perspectives defined by sound bites, propaganda, fears.
And sometimes, when we are afraid,
we may puff up our image of who 'we' are,
and develop a deflated image of who 'they' are.
Help us instead, dear God,
to see the world as you are creating it:
beautiful lands inhabited by brothers and sisters
who are different, who are practising caring for each other,
each one filled with potential.
Help us to see across divisions that we impose,
to resist the urge to create comfortable distances that
make it easy to label the 'other' as strange.
Perhaps we can learn to see 'them' as you do.
Perhaps they are actually a lot like us, after all.
Give us tools to help train our eyes, and hearts.

Today I draw to discover the beauty of Lake Tishreen, Syria.
Amen

expanding perceptions

Were you to come today, God,
you likely wouldn't come knocking on the door of
my suburban home,
even though that fancy wreath dons the door.
It's not even the Holy of holies
where you'd be spending your time, I'm guessing.
Instead, I'm thinking I might find you
down the street,
with our brothers and sisters on the margins.
    Not enough money.
    Not enough education.
    Too much grime and smell.
They take refuge. Hidden. Afraid.
They know their place.

Sadly, I don't know mine.
The place where you lead,
where you call me to dwell,
is right there by their side.

This Advent, knock,
and invite me to walk with you.
Take me where your words of love,
grace and mercy need to be heard,
to be seen in action.
Let me be part of your new heaven and new earth,
all your children courageously working together to
build a new community of God.
One day at a time, one person at a time,
com-passion. Hanging together.
Amen

hanging with outcasts

How we love to expand our reach.
We reach out a hand.
We do outreach in our communities.
Our cities reach out to those in need.
Our country gives assistance when disaster strikes ...

Sometimes though, in our talking, giving, sharing,
we miss the opportunity to truly be with each other,
to learn from each other, to see you in each other.
Why? We fail to develop communications
that invite give and take.
Ways of 'being with'
that help us to know each other,
ways of 'being with'
that help us to see you anew, God.

Be with us in these days.
Help us to reach out not only
with our love and care,
but to extend a space of welcome.
A space of quiet. A space of listening.

There are so many whose voices
we simply don't hear.
Voices that don't come from the centre,
surrounded by lights and mics,
but from the edges.
Beautiful, wise voices.
Silenced.

In these holy days,
may we seek to expand the chorus of voices,
that together we might
invite a new space:
a chorus of people listening to each other
and miraculously hearing your voice anew
in our midst.
Let it be so, O listening God.
Let it be so.
Amen

listening

O God of the universe, of all times and places,
in our humble attempts to honour you,
we name you.
We call you
    Elohim – Creator, Mighty and Strong,
    El Roi – God of Seeing,
    Messiah – Promised Deliverer.
Yet, you are also omnipotent, transcendent,
miraculous.
You are of old, but also of today and tomorrow.
You are our Father. You are our Mother.
How is it, dear God, that you are so near us,
yet God of all?
You know us intimately,
yet we cannot even imagine the greatness of you.
You hold our hand,
yet imagine futures that we cannot fathom.
We call you by name,
but you are beyond any we can offer.

Open our eyes to all that you are
and all that you are becoming.
With hearts so very grateful,
we thank you,
that you invite us to call you ours.
All of ours.
Amen

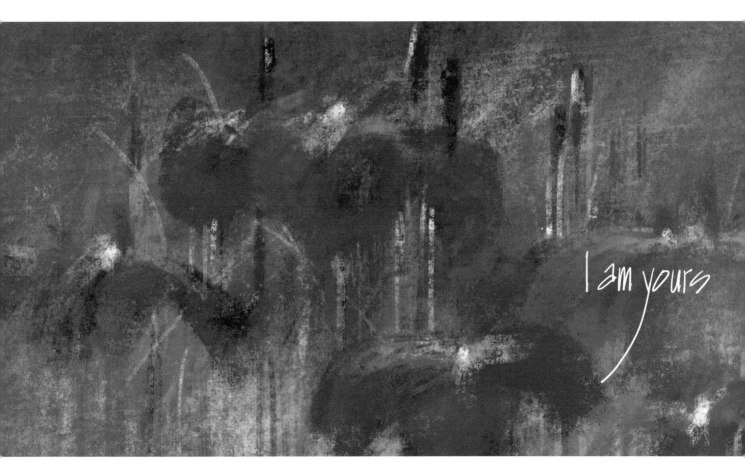

I am yours

God,
in the midst of our ordinary lives –
you break through,
and claim us.
You choose to dwell in and around us,
transforming ordinary spaces,
our ordinary bodies,
our ordinary work,
and making them extraordinary.
Sacred.
Open our eyes to the sacred in and around us,
that we may cherish it,
and cherish these encounters with you.
Holy.
Sacred spaces for you to dwell
with each of your children.
Holy.
Holy.
Holy.
Amen

dwelling in and around you

For ages your voice has spoken of grace and mercy.
It will continue into all our tomorrows.
Remind us today of the many ways that you speak to us still –
through composers, authors, artists,
through pastors, friends and colleagues,
and through brothers and sisters we have yet to meet.
You live in our very midst.
When we listen,
we hear you speak in different languages.
When we pause, our eyes see you uniquely.
When we spend time together, we discover
that our faith stories are as different as we are.
In all this marvellous mix, your breath lives.
And because of this marvellous mix,
you live larger than we can ever imagine.

May your voice continue to be heard in young and old,
near and far, in shouts and whispers,
in Farsi, Arabic, Mandarin – and more,
that we may celebrate its wonder-filled complexity.
Love so large.
Larger and larger still.
Let it be so.
Amen

speaking in many voices

God,
today I draw to pray into being –
safety in the midst of danger,
hope for the desperate,
fear giving way to joy,
silent voices heard,
life, when death is all around,
welcome for the stranger,
an end to tears,
an end to all their tears,
an end to mine.

O God,
you are our hope.
Come quickly.
Come for all your people.
Amen

the voice for the voiceless

Stir up your power, O God,
and come.
Come to change the hearts of our nations.
In a time and place where there is enough –
enough money,
enough food and
a place for everyone –
it seems we must learn anew
what it means to live together.
Teach us to construct a new model,
with policies and practices
that fight fear with radical compassion.
Help us to imagine nations
of grace, of hope, of mercy –
beloved communities.

Stir up our nations' hearts, O God,
that we may become
the people of faith
that you dream we can be.
Fighting for justice.
Generous in love.
Enough for all.
Enough for everyone.
Amen

stirring the nations' hearts

O God,
how we hunger and thirst for love,
for acceptance, for equal footing.
Give us courage to join with our brothers and sisters
to move beyond tolerance, beyond acceptance,
and towards true compassion.
Build among us opportunities for radical compassion
that will move us forward into
the miraculous generosity that you offer each of us.
Draw your people together.
Weave us into wondrous communities of love for all.
There is much work to do.
There is no time to wait.
O, come quickly, Advent God.
Burn brightly.
Swift and strong.
Amen

imagining radical compassion

Avert the gaze.
Turn away.
Watch the screen.
Have a drink. Slam the door.
Avoid the problem.
A go-to solution for discomfort, no?
The distance eases the pain. Numbing, sometimes.
Why is it so hard to open our eyes, to see the truth?
Is it because when we do, we place ourselves
square in the sight lines of another? Vulnerably aligned.
I guess that's the rub. Vulnerability. Empathy. Passion.
In relationship.

O God who calls us into new relationships,
with you and with each other, draw us together.
Make us hungry to know one another.
Hold us together when it's hard.
Open our hearts and minds to new truths.
Be the love that connects us, one to another.
One family. One neighbour. One nation.
One compassionate people of God.
Let it be so, O God.
Let it be so.
Amen

O God, beyond our understanding,
you are of all time and all space.
Miraculously, you are also with each of us.
All your children,
and not just today, but always,
from generation to generation.
Know that our gratitude is simply beyond measure.
Amen

I am with you always

As we move into these last days
preparing for your Advent, dear God,
we ask to feel your presence surrounding us.
We long to know you,
to be fully immersed in your great love.
May our senses delight in the
sights, smells, sounds, tastes and touch
of your coming.
Tangible graces.
For all your people.
Amen

surrounding you

It's our people we long to be with, right?
These are invited. Those are not.
These are tagged and friended. Those are not.
Our worlds can easily grow so small.
In this season of generosity, we pray, O God,
that you expand our sense of community
beyond our comfort zones.
Break through the protective walls we build.
Open our eyes to the larger landscape of mutuality.
Cast fears aside and build
safe spaces of shared vulnerability,
where we lean on each other, growing stronger together.
Kinetic, changing, messy, yes,
but glorious. Simply glorious.
Connect us one to another with threads of
grace, love and mercy.
Together, may we become
the Beloved Community that
you dream we can be.
Amen*

* An animation reveals the drawing process of this piece: https://youtu.be/7MUHdEk7qOg

connecting

O God,
you have spoken to and through
your people for thousands of years.
Holy texts tell us of ways in which you have acted
in the lives of all your people.
You have nourished your people,
delivered your people, taught us compassion.

Story after story recounts your love.
Stories told from one generation to the next.
In word and image, your Spirit lives.
Creating. Redeeming. Sanctifying.
Making us whole.

With your coming Advent,
we boldly ask you to continue to
speak through all your people.
May we listen,
and may we bear witness to your love,
your grace,
your gifts.
Into a chaotic world you came.
Into our chaotic world you promise to come
again and again.
Let it be so, dear God.
Let it be so.
Amen

for I have brought you out of the land of Egypt

O God,
you continue to give us gifts beyond measure.
And in the midst of this bounty,
you say 'Go.'
Go with these gifts.
Go with my love,
and be my hands and feet in a world
so desperately in need.

Dearest God,
as you come to us in these holy days,
open our eyes to see you anew in our midst.
Open our ears to hear your gentle call.
Open our hearts that we might
receive the love that you so gently offer as we go.
Then may we, your people sent,
work together in both body and spirit
to become a bit more like the Beloved Community
that you dream we can be.
In these holiest of days,
let it be so, dear loving God.
Let it be so.
Amen

Do as I have done

Onto this corner,
this street,
into this neighbourhood,
this home,
into these hands,
and in hands around the globe,
we ask that you come.
Be born in us today.
All of us.
Be born anew,
and change the world.
Amen
Amen
Amen

for today my light is born in you

O beloved child of God,
bearing the light of Christmas,
today, God calls your name.
Here, just as you are,
God's love enfolds you.
May you step forward boldly,
knowing you are named and claimed,
cherished beyond measure.
May your open eyes delight
in the miracle and wonder
of Christ's light and love –
gifts for all the earth.

Happy Christmas.